Mastering Marketing: The Ultimate Guide to Crafting Winning Plans

Barnett Nicholas

COPYRIGHT

About The Author

Hey there!

I'm Nicholas Barnett, and I'm super excited to share with you my latest creation, "Mastering Market: Nicholas Barnett's Blueprint for Marketing Success."

You know, I've spent a good chunk of my career in the fast-paced world of marketing, and boy, has it been a ride! From diving into the intricacies of market forces to steering through the twists and turns of consumer behavior, every step has been a lesson.

"Mastering Market " is not just a book to me; it's a labor of love—a collection of all the insights, victories, and occasional setbacks that have shaped my journey. Whether you're a seasoned marketer or just starting, I wanted to create something that could be your go-to guide for navigating the ever-shifting tides of the business world.

I graduated from the Sloan School of Management, and from there, it's been a rollercoaster of experiences—leading marketing teams, crafting strategies, and being in the thick of it all. This book is like a conversation we'd have over coffee, where I spill the beans on what it takes to not just survive but thrive in the dynamic landscape of marketing.

Beyond the pages of this book, I've had the incredible opportunity to stand on stages around the world, sharing my thoughts on the future of marketing, brand resilience, and how to stay ahead in this crazy, fast-paced industry. And you know what? It's been a blast!

But it's not just about me. I'm passionate about giving back and helping the next generation of marketers find their footing. That's why mentorship and sharing knowledge are so close to my heart. We're all in this together, right?

So, here's to "Mastering Market" and to you—fellow marketer, entrepreneur, or anyone curious about the magic that happens behind the scenes. Let's embark on this journey together, and may the insights within these pages guide you to success in the ever-evolving world of marketing!

Mastering Marketing

Table of Contents

Chapter 9: marketing Schedules and Arranging Your Activities

- The Meaning of Marketing Schedules
- Building Your Marketing Schedule
- Instruments and Programming
- Adjusting Consistency and Adaptability

Conclusion

- Wrapping

Reviews

Upsell

INTRODUCTION

Navigating the Marketing Landscape

In a world driven by rapid technological advancements, shifting consumer behaviors, and ever-evolving market dynamics, mastering the art and science of marketing is more crucial than ever.

Welcome to **"Mastering Marketing:** A Comprehensive Guide to Effective Strategies," where we embark on a journey through the multifaceted realm of marketing plans, strategies, and tactics.

The Importance of Marketing Plans

Marketing is the lifeblood of any business, whether you're a startup striving to make your mark or an established enterprise aiming to maintain your competitive edge. At its core, marketing is about connecting with your audience, understanding their needs, and delivering value in ways that resonate. However, Success in marketing is not a matter of chance; it's a result of deliberate planning and execution.

Marketing plans are the compass that guides organizations toward their goals.

They provide clarity, direction, and focus, enabling businesses to chart a course toward success.

 A well-crafted
A marketing plan is not merely a document; it's a strategic tool that aligns marketing efforts with broader business objectives.

Defining Your Marketing Goals

Every marketing journey begins with a destination in mind. In this book, we will explore the critical first step in crafting effective marketing plans: setting clear and actionable marketing objectives. Without well-defined
goals, marketing efforts lack direction and purpose.
We will delve into the art of crafting objectives that are SMART (Specific, Measurable,
Achievable, Relevant, and Time-bound), providing the foundation upon which your marketing strategy will be built.

Understanding Your Target Audience

In the realm of marketing, understanding your audience is akin to unlocking a treasure trove of opportunities. Chapter by chapter, we will guide you through the process of identifying and comprehending your target audience—the individuals or businesses most likely to benefit from your products or services. By crafting detailed buyer personas and conducting thorough audience research, you'll gain insights that will shape your marketing strategies and tactics.

Crafting a Winning Marketing Strategy

Effective marketing is not about chasing trends or blindly copying competitors; it's about creating strategies that align with your unique business goals and resonate with your audience. Throughout this book, we will explore the art of developing marketing strategies that set you apart, resonate with your audience, and drive results.

In the digital age, data and analytics play a pivotal role in marketing success.
 We will discuss the importance of data-driven decision-making, explore the tools and techniques for gathering valuable insights, and provide guidance on how to leverage data to refine and optimize your marketing efforts.
As we embark on this journey together, our goal is to equip you with the knowledge, tools, and strategies to navigate the ever-changing marketing landscape with confidence. Whether you're a seasoned marketing professional seeking to sharpen your skills or a newcomer eager to master the fundamentals, "Mastering Marketing" is your comprehensive guide to success.

Are you ready to embark on this exciting journey through the world of marketing plans and strategies? Let's dive in and discover the art and science of effective marketing.

Chapter 1: Setting Your Marketing Objectives

In the realm of promotion, achievement starts with a reasonable internal compass. Similarly, as a boat needs an objective, your showcasing endeavors need targets—clear, explicit, and quantifiable objectives that guide your methodology and activities. In this section, we investigate the basic significance of setting promotional targets and how to successfully create them.

The Importance of Clear Objectives

Advertising targets act as the establishment whereupon your whole marketing plan is constructed. They give you concentration, reason, and a guide for your showcasing exercises. Clear and distinct goals are fundamental in light of multiple factors:

1. **Direction:** Goals offer an exact comprehension of what you intend to accomplish, assisting your group with remaining focused.

2. **Alignment with Business Goals:** Powerful advertising targets line up with more extensive business objectives, guaranteeing that your promoting endeavors add to the general progress of your association.

3. **Measurability:** Very well-created goals are quantifiable, permitting you to follow progress and assess the outcome of your promotional efforts.

4. Accountability: Targets give a premise to responsibility, doling out liability regarding accomplishing explicit results.

5. Decision-Making: Clear targets guide direction by assisting you with focusing on promoting exercises and apportioning assets successfully.

Creating Your Marketing Goals

Viable Marketing goals are, in many cases, brilliant—explicit, quantifiable, achievable, persistent, and time-bound. We should separate every part.

Specific: Goals ought to be exact and itemized. Stay away from obscure proclamations and go for the gold. For instance, rather than saying, "Increment deals," a particular goal may be,

"Increment month-to-month deals income by 15%."

Measurable: Your targets ought to be quantifiable, with the goal that you can gauge progress and achievement. Use measurements, for example, rates, dollar sums, or client counts, to make your targets quantifiable.

Achievable: Goals ought to be practical and feasible. Put forth objectives that challenge your group yet stay within the domain of probability. Ridiculous targets can prompt disappointment and demotivation.

Relevant: Guarantee that your targets are lined up with your business objectives and the ongoing business sector climate. They ought to seem OK concerning your industry, crowd, and assets.

Time-bound: Set a particular time for accomplishing your goals. Without cutoff times, there's less desperation and responsibility. For instance, "Increment site traffic by 20% in six months or less."

Crafting Your Marketing Objectives

Showcasing targets can include different classifications, contingent upon your business' necessities and objectives. A few normal classifications include:

1. Sales and Revenue: Targets connected with expanding deals, income, piece of the pie, or net revenues.

2. Customer Acquisition: Objectives pointed toward gaining new clients or extending your client base.

3. Customer Retention: Goals zeroed in on holding existing clients and encouraging devotion.

4. Brand Awareness: Objectives connected with expanding brand permeability, acknowledgment, and review among your interest group

5. Lead Generation: Targets for creating qualified leads for your items or administrations

6. Content Engagement: Objectives connected with content advertising, for example, expanding site traffic, blog commitment, or online entertainment supporters.

7. Product Launch: Targets revolved around sending off another item or administration effectively.

Model Shrewd Showcasing Targets

1. Objective: increase month-to-month traffic.
Shrewd Objective: Increase month-to-month site traffic by 20% throughout the following half

year by carrying out happy promotion and Search engine optimization systems.

2. Objective: Lift client degrees of consistency.

Brilliant Objective: Further develop client consistency standards by 10% within the following quarter by carrying out a client steadfastness program and customized correspondence.

3. Objective: Send off another item effectively.

Brilliant Objective: Accomplish $50,000 in deal income within the main month after the item is sent off by carrying out a multi-channel showcasing effort.

Setting clear and brilliant advertising targets is the pivotal initial phase in making a powerful showcasing plan. These targets give bearing and motivation to your advertising endeavors, guaranteeing that each activity adds to your general business objectives.

As we push ahead in this book, we'll investigate how to foster methodologies and strategies that line up with your advertising targets, transforming your arrangements into quantifiable triumphs.

How about we proceed with our excursion into dominating advertising by investigating crowd ID and the specialty of creating convincing purchaser personas in the following part?

Chapter 2: Target audience identification

In the realm of promotion, understanding your crowd is similar to opening a gold mine of chances. Part by section, we will direct you through the method involved with distinguishing and appreciating your interest group—the people or organizations probably going to profit from your items or administrations.

By making definite purchaser personas and leading careful crowd research, you'll acquire bits of knowledge that will shape your advertising techniques and

Understanding what Your Listeners might be thinking

Your crowd is at the core of your showcasing endeavors. They are the people or associations you plan to reach, draw in, and convert into faithful clients. Understanding your crowd is significant in light of multiple factors:

1. Personalization: Understanding what your listeners might be thinking permits you to tailor your advertising messages and content to resonate with their inclinations, needs, and trouble spots.

2. Relevance: Viable showcasing is tied in with conveying the right message to the ideal individuals brilliantly.
Crowd understanding guarantees that your advertising endeavors stay pertinent.

3. Efficiency: Designated showcasing saves time and assets. By zeroing in on your ideal crowd, you can try not to squander assets on less important socioeconomics.

4. Competitive Advantage: A profound comprehension of your crowd can be an upper hand, assisting you with separating your image and items on the lookout.

Creating Buyer Personas

Purchaser personas are semi-fictitious portrayals of your optimal clients.

They typify the qualities, ways of behaving, and inclinations of the people or organizations you are probably going to draw in with your image.

Creating point-by-point purchaser personas includes:

1. Research: Accumulate information and experiences through studies, meetings, and statistical surveying to better comprehend your ebb and flow and potential clients.

2. Segmentation: Distinguish shared traits and examples in your crowd information to bunch clients into portions that share comparative qualities.

3. Persona Creation: Foster personas that address each portion. Give them names, portrayals, and histories that acculturate them.

4. Persona Details: Determine segment data, objectives, challenges, values, inclinations, and trouble spots for every persona.

5. Situation Mapping: Consider how every persona could interface with your image, from the underlying disclosure stage to turning into an unwavering client.

Conducting Audience Research

Crowd research is a continuous cycle that includes gathering information and experiences about your interest group. Key advances include:

1. Overviews and Questionnaires: Make reviews to accumulate criticism and inclinations from your crowd. Use devices like web-based reviews, email polls, or input structures.

2. Web-based Entertainment Insights: Dissect information from your virtual entertainment channels to acquire insights into the socioeconomics and ways of behaving of your devotees and connecting with clients.

3. Site Analytics: Use web investigation apparatuses like Google Examination to follow guest conduct, socioeconomics, and interests on your site.

4. Client Interviews: Direct one-on-one meetings with existing clients to acquire a more profound comprehension of their requirements, inspirations, and encounters with your image.

5. Contender Analysis: Explore your rivals to recognize shared characteristics in their client base and find amazing open doors for separation

Refining Your Marketing Strategy

Whenever you have made point-by-point purchaser personas and led crowd research, you can fit your showcasing systems and messages to address the particular requirements and inclinations of every persona. This designated approach upgrades the pertinence and viability of your showcasing endeavors.

Understanding your ideal interest group is a key stage in dominating promotion. By making itemized purchaser personas and directing crowd research, you gain important bits of knowledge that illuminate your advertising methodologies and strategies.

Chapter 3: Market Research and Analysis

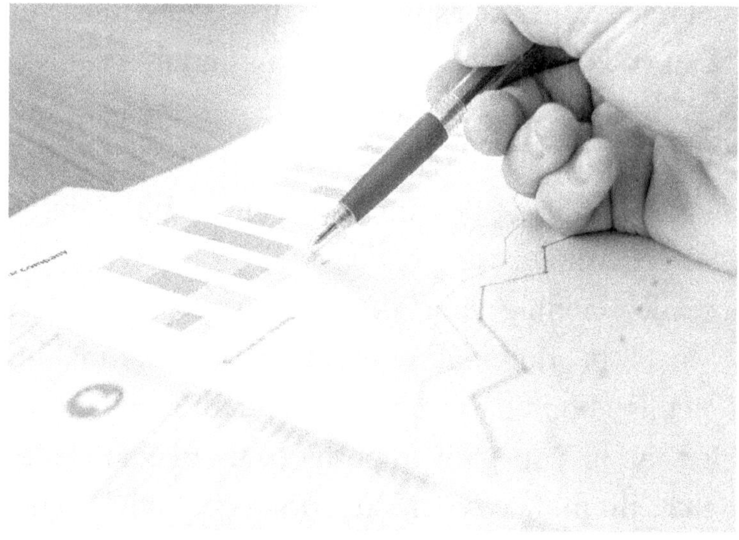

In the world of marketing, knowledge is power. Market research and analysis provide the knowledge you need to make informed decisions, identify opportunities, and create strategies that resonate with your target audience.

In this chapter, we explore the significance of market research, the types of research available, and the steps involved in conducting effective market analysis.

The Role of Market Research

Market research is the systematic process of gathering, analyzing, and interpreting data about your market, industry, and target audience. It serves several critical functions in marketing:

1. Understanding Market Trends: Market research helps you stay up-to-date with industry trends, consumer preferences, and emerging market shifts.

2. Identifying Opportunities and Gaps: By analyzing market data, you can identify unmet needs, gaps in the market, and opportunities for innovation.

3. Audience Insights: Market research provides insights into your target audience's behavior, preferences, and pain points, enabling you to tailor your marketing efforts effectively.

4. Competitor Analysis: You can gain a competitive edge by studying your competitors, understanding their strategies, and identifying areas where you can differentiate.

5. Risk Mitigation: Research helps you anticipate potential challenges and risks, allowing you to proactively address them in your marketing plans

Types of Market Research

Market research can take various forms, depending on
your objectives and the information you seek.
Common types of market research include:

1. Descriptive Research: Descriptive research aims to describe the characteristics and attributes of a market or audience. It provides a snapshot of current conditions.

2. Exploratory Research: Exploratory research seeks to explore a problem or phenomenon, often in the absence of clear research objectives. It's a valuable starting point for identifying research questions.

3. Causal Research: Causal research investigates cause-and-effect relationships.

It explores how changes in one variable (such as marketing activities) affect another (customer behavior).

4. Qualitative Research: Qualitative research involves gathering non-numerical data, often through methods like interviews, focus groups, or open-ended surveys. It helps uncover insights, motivations, and attitudes.

5. Quantitative Research: Quantitative research focuses on collecting numerical data that can be Analyzed statistically.
It involves surveys, experiments, and structured data collection.

The Market Research Process

Effective market research involves a structured process to ensure that you gather relevant and accurate information. The steps in the market research process typically include:

1. Define Objectives: Clearly define the objectives and goals of your research.
 What specific information are you seeking to uncover?

2. Data Collection: Choose the appropriate methods for collecting data, whether through surveys, interviews, observational studies, or secondary sources like industry reports.

3. Data Analysis: Analyze the collected data to identify patterns, trends, and insights. Use statistical tools and software as needed.

4. Interpretation: Interpret the data in the context of your marketing objectives.
 What do the findings mean for your marketing strategy?

5. Actionable Insights: Extract actionable insights from your research findings. What Strategies or tactics can you implement based on the data?

6. Reporting: Prepare a comprehensive report or presentation summarizing your research process, findings, and recommendations.

7. Implementation: Use the insights gained from research to inform your marketing plans and campaigns. Ensure that your actions align with the research findings.

8. Monitor and Iterate: Continuously monitor market conditions, consumer behavior, and industry trends.
Be prepared to iterate your strategies based on new data and changing
circumstances.

Ethical Considerations in Market Research

Ethical conduct is paramount in market research. Respect for privacy, transparency in data collection, and fair treatment of participants are fundamental principles. Always obtain informed consent from participants, protect their personal information, and ensure that your research complies with applicable laws and regulations.

Market research and analysis are invaluable tools in the marketer's toolbox. They provide the insights and data needed to make informed decisions, craft effective marketing strategies, and remain competitive in a dynamic market landscape.

In the chapters that follow, we'll explore how to use these insights to perform competitive analysis, refine your marketing strategies, and execute successful marketing campaigns.

Let's continue our journey of mastering marketing by delving into competitive analysis and positioning in the next chapter

Chapter 4: Competitive Analysis and Positioning

Understanding your rivals and situating your image in the market are fundamental stages in creating an effective promotion plan. In this part, we investigate the force of cutthroat examination, the devices, and procedures for acquiring bits of knowledge about your rivals, and the specialty of situating your image for the most extreme effect.

The Power of Competitive Analysis

Cutthroat investigation is the method involved with social events and assessing data about your rivals. It provides important experiences that illuminate your advertising systems and strategies. Powerful, aggressive examination offers a few benefits:

1. Identifying Qualities and Weaknesses: By concentrating on your rivals, you can distinguish their assets and shortcomings, permitting you to exploit open doors and relieve dangers.

 2. Market Opportunities: Examination assists you with recognizing holes on the lookout and regions where your image can tolerate outings.

3. Benchmarking: Cutthroat examination gives benchmarks against which you can gauge your presentation.

4. Differentiation: By understanding your rivals, you can create an interesting incentive that separates your image.

The Competitive Analysis Framework

An organized way to deal with serious examination includes the accompanying key parts:

1. Recognizing Competitors: Start by distinguishing your immediate and roundabout contenders. Direct contenders offer comparative items or services, while circuitous contenders might address comparative requirements through various means.

2. Contender Profiles: Make profiles for every contender, including their set of experiences, items or administrations, a portion of the overall industry, qualities, shortcomings, and vital needs.

3. SWOT Analysis: Play out a SWOT examination (Qualities, Shortcomings, Potential Open Doors, and Dangers) for every contender. This structure assists you with distinguishing inward and outside factors that influence their prosperity.

4. Cutthroat Positioning: Determine how every contender positions themselves on the lookout. What remarkable worth do they offer, and how would they impart it to their crowd?

5. Showcasing Strategies: Dissect your rivals' promoting methodologies, including their informing, publicizing channels, content advertising, and web-based entertainment presence.

6. Client Feedback: Accumulate client input and audits about your rivals' items or administrations. What do clients like or dislike about them?

7. Evaluating Strategies: Comprehend how contenders value their items or administrations and whether they offer limits, advancements, or steadfastness programs

Positioning Your Brand

The position has the specialty of characterizing how your brand needs to be seen in the personalities of your ideal interest group. Viable positioning empowers you to separate your brand and create an exceptional character.
Key stages in positioning your brand include:

1. Interest group alignment: guarantee that your image lines up with the inclinations and requirements of your interest group.
It ought to impact them and address their trouble spots.

2. One-of-a-kind Selling Recommendation (USP): Characterize your image's novel selling points. What separates your image from your rivals? For what reason should clients pick you?

3. Brand Personality: Art a brand character that matches your situation. Is your image agreeable, imaginative, dependable, or rich?
The character ought to be predictable across all touchpoints.

4. Brand Messaging: Foster clear and convincing information that imparts your image's worth and reverberates with your crowd.

This information ought to be obvious in your showcasing materials and missions.

5. Consistency: Keep up with consistency in your image's visual personality, information, and tone across all promotional channels and materials.

Applying Competitive Insights

Whenever you've led a cutthroat investigation and characterized your image situation, you can Apply these bits of knowledge to your advertising plan.

Tailor your procedures and information to stress your assets and separate your image from rivals. Cutthroat investigation and positioning are essential components of a fruitful showcasing plan.

By understanding your rivals and decisively situating your image, you can formulate promoting techniques that reverberate with your ideal interest group.

 fabricate brand dedication, and drive outcomes in the serious commercial center.

In the parts that follow, we'll keep on investigating the fundamental arts of dominating and promoting, including marking, narrating, and item improvement, and that's only the tip of the iceberg.

Chapter 5: Branding and Storytelling

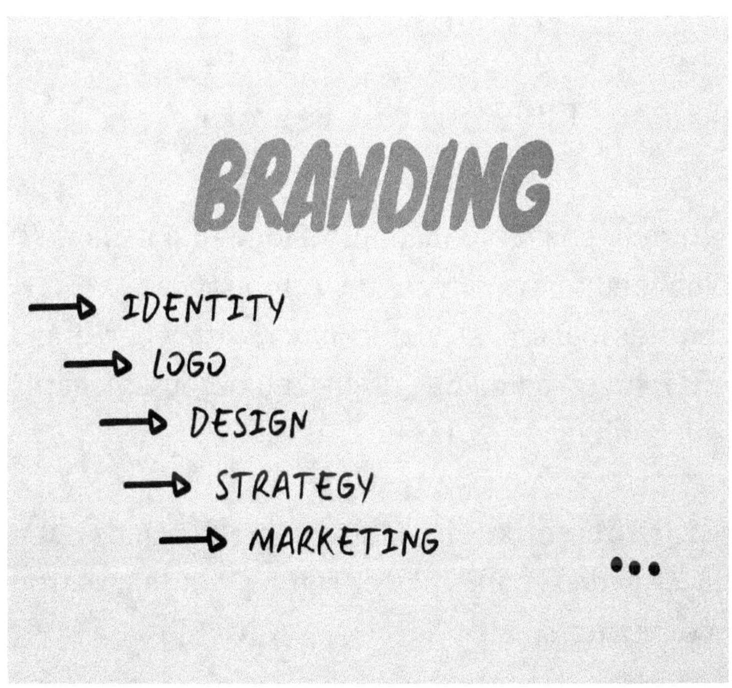

Branding and storytelling are potent tools in the marketer's arsenal. They enable you to create a unique identity, connect with your audience on a deeper level, and leave a lasting impression. In this chapter, we explore the power of branding and storytelling in marketing and how to harness them effectively.

The Power of Branding

Branding is more than just a logo or a name; it's the total of the perceptions, emotions,
and associations people have with your brand. Effective branding offers numerous benefits, including:

1. Differentiation: A strong brand stands out in a crowded marketplace, setting you apart from competitors.

2. Trust and Loyalty: Brands that consistently deliver on their promises build trust and loyalty with their customers.

3. Emotional Connection: A well-crafted brand can evoke emotions and create a personal connection with your audience.

4. Recognition: A strong brand is easily recognizable and memorable, even in a sea of choices.

5. Value Perception: A powerful brand can command higher prices, as customers often associate it with quality and reliability.

Creating Your Brand Identity

Building a strong brand begins with defining your brand identity—a set of attributes and values that represent your brand. Key components of brand identity include:

1. Brand Name: Choose a name that reflects your brand's essence and resonates with your target audience.

2. Logo and Visual Elements: Create a distinctive logo, color palette, and design elements that visually represent your brand.

3. Brand Voice: Define your brand's tone, style, and language. Is your brand casual, formal, friendly, or authoritative?

4. Values and Mission: Articulate your brand's core values and mission. What does your brand stand for, and what are your guiding principles?

5. Target Audience: Understand your target audience deeply. Tailor your brand identity to align with their preferences and needs.

6. Brand Story: Craft a compelling brand story that communicates your history, values, and journey. Storytelling humanizes your brand and makes it relatable.

The Art of Storytelling

Storytelling is a powerful tool for connecting with your audience emotionally and conveying your brand's message effectively. Effective storytelling involves:

1. Relatability: Craft stories that your audience can relate to, highlighting challenges, triumphs, and shared values.

2. Emotion: Use storytelling to evoke emotions. Whether it's joy, empathy, or inspiration, emotions create memorable experiences.

3. Consistency: Maintain consistency in your brand's storytelling across various channels and touchpoints.

4. Simplicity: Keep your stories simple and easy to understand. Avoid jargon or complexity that might alienate your audience.

5. Authenticity: Authenticity is key in storytelling. Be truthful and genuine in your narratives to build trust.

Applying Branding and Storytelling in Marketing

Once you've defined your brand identity and crafted compelling stories, it's time to apply them to your marketing efforts. Your branding and storytelling should resonate through:

1. Content Marketing: Infuse your content, whether it's blog posts, videos, or social media updates, with your brand's voice and stories.

2. Visual Identity: Use your brand's visual elements consistently in all marketing materials and campaigns.

3. Customer Experiences: Ensure that your brand's values and stories are reflected in every customer interaction.

4. Advertising: Craft advertising campaigns that align with your brand identity and convey compelling narratives.

5. Social Media: Leverage social media platforms to share your brand stories and engage with your audience.

Branding and storytelling are powerful tools that can elevate your marketing efforts to new heights. A strong brand identity and compelling stories create an emotional connection with your audience, differentiate your brand, and build trust and loyalty.

In the chapters that follow, we'll explore other critical aspects of mastering marketing, including product development, innovation, and the elements of a comprehensive marketing plan.

Let's continue our journey by delving into the intricacies of product development and innovation in Chapter 6.

Chapter 6: Item Improvement and Innovation

In the present powerful business scene, item improvement and advancement are not simply upper hands; they're methods for surviving.

In this part, we dive into the transaction between item improvement and advertising, the item advancement process, and the significance of development in remaining on the ball.

The Exchange Among Items and Promoting

Compelling promotion starts with an item or administration that addresses the issues and wants of your interest group. Item improvement and showcasing are intrinsically interwoven, with each impacting the other:

1. Product-Driven Approach: An item-driven approach begins with making an important contribution, and promoting follows to convey its advantages.

2. Market-Driven Approach: A market-driven approach starts with understanding client needs and inclinations,
driving item improvement to satisfy those prerequisites.

3. Feedback Loop: Item improvement and promotion ought to keep a continuous input circle.

Promoting bits of knowledge illuminates item enhancements, and item execution information guides advertising techniques.

The Item Advancement Cycle

Fruitful item improvement includes an organized interaction that guarantees your contributions line up with market needs. The phases of the item advancement process normally include:

1. Thought Generation: Create and conceptualize thoughts for new items or upgrades to existing
ones. Thoughts can emerge out of client criticism, market patterns, or inward advancement.

2. Thought Screening: Assess and screen thoughts to decide their attainability and arrangement with your business objectives and market requests.
Focus on the most encouraging ideas.

3. Idea Improvement and Testing: Foster point-by-point item ideas and direct market testing to accumulate criticism and refine the thoughts further.

4. Business Analysis: Survey the monetary practicality of the item, taking into account expenses, estimating, and income projections.
Decide if the item lines up with your financial plan and business goals.

5. Model Development: Make models or least practical items (MVPs) to test usefulness and accumulate client criticism.

6. Item Improvement and Testing: Start full-scale item advancement, testing usefulness, quality, and ease of use at each stage.

7. Market Testing: Direct market tests with a select gathering of clients to assess the item's presentation and accumulate experiences for possible upgrades.

8. Commercialization: Get ready for the item's send-off, including advertising methodologies, dissemination, and deals channels.

9. Launch: Formally acquaint the item with the market through different channels, publicizing, and limited-time exercises.

10. Post-Send-off Evaluation: Consistently screen the item's presentation, accumulate client input, and make vital enhancements or changes.

Development as an Upper hand

Advancement isn't restrictedl to item improvement; it reaches out to all parts of your business, from promoting methodologies to client support.

Embracing advancement offers a few advantages:

1. Competitive Edge: Imaginative items and approaches can give you a huge edge on the lookout.

2. Market Responsiveness: Advancement empowers you to respond rapidly to changing economic situations and client requests.

3. Sustainability: Consistent advancement helps your business adjust and flourish in the long haul.

4. Customer Engagement: Creative items and encounters can connect with and enamor your clients, cultivating dedication.

5. Efficiency: Development can smooth out inner cycles, making your business more proficient and savvy.

Applying Item Improvement and Development in Promoting

Integrating item improvement and advancement into your promotion procedure includes:

1. Client-Driven Marketing: Adjust advertising to client necessities and inclinations, accentuating how your inventive items address those issues.

2. Imparting Innovation: Feature the creative parts of your items and how they benefit clients.

3. Agility: Be prepared to adjust showcasing techniques and missions as new items and upgrades are created.

4. Storytelling: Specialty convincing accounts around your creative items and how they take care of true issues.

5. Criticism Loops: Keep up with open channels for client input and use them to illuminate both item advancement and promotion methodologies.

Item improvement and advancement are not just about making new things; they're tied in with tackling issues and meeting the always-developing necessities of your crowd. While showcasing lines of inventive items, it creates a strong collaboration that can drive your image forward.

In the sections that follow, we'll keep on investigating the basic components of dominating promotion, including the components of a thorough showcasing plan and spending plan distribution.

We should continue with Chapter 7, where we'll dive into the basics of showcasing, arranging, and methodology.

Chapter 7: The Components of a Marketing Plan

A showcasing plan is a guide that directs your promoting endeavors, guaranteeing they line up with your business objectives and reverberate with your interest group. In this part, we investigate the critical components of a thorough promotion plan and how to think up a procedure that drives achievement.

The Reason for a Marketing Plan

A showcasing plan serves a few fundamental capabilities in your business:

1. Clarity: It gives a reasonable and reported technique for your showcasing endeavors, guaranteeing everybody in your group figures out their jobs and goals.

2. Focus: A promotion plan assists you with focusing on showcasing exercises, guaranteeing assets are designated successfully.

3. Alignment: It adjusts advertising endeavors to more extensive business goals, guaranteeing that showcasing adds to the general progress of your association.

4.   Measurement: A showcasing plan incorporates measurements and key execution

pointers (KPIs) that permit you to gauge the progress of your promoting efforts.

Key Components of a Marketing Plan

An extensive promotion plan ordinarily incorporates the accompanying key components:

1. Chief Summary: A compact outline of the whole showcasing plan, featuring the principal objectives and systems.

2. Circumstance Analysis: An evaluation of the ongoing economic situation, including a SWOT examination (Qualities, Shortcomings, Potential Open Doors, Dangers) and a cutthroat investigation.

3. Ideal interest group and Purchaser Personas: An itemized portrayal of your interest group, including purchaser personas and their qualities

4. Promoting Objectives: Clear, explicit, quantifiable, attainable, important, and time-bound (Shrewd) goals that guide your showcasing endeavors

5. Promoting Strategies: The significant level procedures you'll use to accomplish your goals, for example, happy showcasing, online entertainment advertising, or email advertising.

6. Strategic Plans: Explicit strategies and activity plans for carrying out your systems, including timetables, obligations, and spending plans.

7. Spending plan Allocation: A breakdown of your showcasing spending plan, specifying how will be distributed to different strategies and missions.

8. Content Calendar: A timetable framing the substance and promoting exercises you'll execute consistently.

9. Measurements and KPIs: A rundown of key execution pointers (KPIs) and measurements that will be utilized to gauge the progress of your promoting endeavors.

10. Risk Assessment: An assessment of expected dangers and difficulties that could influence your marketing plan, alongside alternate courses of action.

11. Execution Timeline: A course of events illustrating how each showcasing strategy will be executed.

12. Checking and Evaluation: An arrangement for continuous observation of your showcasing exercises, alongside a timetable for considering the outcomes in contrast to your goals

Making Your Marketing Plan

To make a far-reaching marketing plan, follow these means:

1. Characterize Your Objectives: Begin by setting clear and explicit promotion targets that line up with your business objectives.

2. Figure out Your Audience: Lead intensive exploration to grasp your interest group, their requirements, inclinations, and trouble spots.

3. Pick Your Strategies: Select advertising systems that are probably going to assist you with accomplishing your targets in light of your crowd and industry.

4. Create Strategic Plans: Make definite activity plans for every procedure, indicating timetables, obligations, and spending plans.

5. Designate Resources: Decide how your advertising financial plan will be distributed

across different strategies and missions.

6. Make a Substance Calendar: Foster a substance schedule that frames what content will be created and when it will be distributed.

7. Screen and Adjust: Consistently screen your marketing endeavors, track KPIs, and be ready to change your strategies and systems because of execution information.

8. Impart and Educate: Guarantee that your whole group knows about the showcasing plan and grasps their jobs and obligations.

A very organized marketing plan is the foundation of compelling promotion. It is the guide that directs your endeavors, guaranteeing they are engaged, aligned with your business goals, and quantifiable.

By cautiously making every component of your showcasing plan, you'll be better prepared to explore the intricate scene of promoting and making progress.

In the parts that follow, we'll investigate extra parts of dominating showcasing, including planning, advertising schedules, and keeping up with consistency in your endeavors.

We should proceed with our excursion in Part 8, where we'll investigate the basic subject of planning and asset portion in advertising.

Chapter 8: Budgeting and Resource Allocation in Marketing

Effective budgeting and resource allocation are pivotal for achieving your marketing objectives while maximizing the return on investment (ROI) of your marketing efforts. In this chapter, we delve into the strategies and considerations for budgeting and allocating resources effectively in your marketing plan.

The Importance of Budgeting

A well-defined marketing budget serves as a financial roadmap for your marketing efforts, providing numerous benefits:

1. Resource Allocation: It ensures that you allocate resources efficiently, directing them toward the most impactful marketing activities.

2. Control: A budget helps you control expenses and prevent overspending, ensuring that your marketing efforts remain within financial limits.

3. ROI Measurement: It allows you to measure the return on investment (ROI) of your marketing campaigns, helping you assess their effectiveness.

4. Alignment: A budget aligns marketing activities with your overall business goals, ensuring that every dollar spent contributes to your company's success.

Setting Your Marketing Budget

Determining the appropriate marketing budget for your business requires a thoughtful and data-driven approach. Consider the following steps:

1. Assess Your Financials: Review your business's financial situation, taking into account revenue, profit margins, and other financial metrics.

2. Set Clear Objectives: Define your marketing objectives and the strategies needed to achieve them. Different objectives may require varying levels of investment.

3. Industry Benchmarks: Research industry benchmarks to gain insights into typical marketing budget ranges for businesses similar to yours.

4. Past Performance: Analyze your past marketing performance to identify which strategies delivered the best ROI and consider allocating more resources to those areas.

5. Competitive Analysis: Study your competitors to understand their marketing efforts and budgets. While not definitive, this can provide a benchmark for your budget.

6. Marketing Mix: Consider the mix of marketing channels and tactics you plan to employ. Different channels have varying costs associated with them.

7. Scalability: Ensure that your budget is scalable, meaning you can adjust it as needed based on changing circumstances and opportunities.

8. Testing and Optimization: Allocate a portion of your budget for testing and optimizing campaigns to improve efficiency over time.

Allocating Resources Effectively

Once you've set your marketing budget, the next step is to allocate resources effectively to achieve your marketing objectives. Consider these **strategies:**

1. Prioritize High-Impact Activities: Focus on marketing activities that have a proven track record of delivering results and align with your objectives.

2. Balanced Allocation: Allocate resources across different marketing channels to diversify your reach and reduce risk.

3. Flexibility: Be prepared to reallocate resources during the year if certain strategies are underperforming or if new opportunities arise.

4. Measurement and Analytics: Invest in measurement tools and analytics to track the performance of your marketing activities and make data-driven decisions.

5. Marketing ROI: Continuously monitor the ROI of each marketing campaign and tactic, adjusting resource allocation accordingly.

6. Marketing Technology: Invest in marketing technology and automation tools to improve efficiency and effectiveness.

Adjusting Your Budget

Marketing is not static, and market conditions can change rapidly. Be prepared to adjust your budget and resource allocation as needed. Reasons for adjustment may include:

1. Market Changes: If market conditions shift, such as changes in customer behavior or competitive landscape, be prepared to adapt your budget and strategies.

2. Performance Insights: Use performance data and analytics to identify underperforming areas and reallocate resources to high-performing ones.

3. New Opportunities: When new marketing opportunities or emerging trends arise, be flexible enough to allocate resources to explore them.

4. Seasonal Variations: Adjust your budget seasonally to accommodate variations in demand or consumer behavior.

Budgeting and resource allocation are fundamental aspects of mastering marketing. A well-structured budget and thoughtful allocation of resources ensure that your marketing efforts remain on track, deliver results, and provide a clear path to achieving your business objectives. By maintaining flexibility and continuously monitoring performance, you'll be well-equipped to adapt to changing market dynamics and opportunities.

Chapter 9: marketing Schedules and Arranging Your Activities

A very organized marketing schedule is the key part that holds your showcasing plan together. It gives structure, assists you with remaining coordinated, and guarantees that your promotional exercises are executed in a convenient and composed way. In this part, we investigate the significance of advertising schedules and how to design your showcasing exercises successfully after some time.

The Meaning of Marketing Schedules

A marketing schedule fills in as a visual portrayal of your showcasing plan throughout a particular time, generally a year or a quarter. It offers a few benefits:

1. Organization: It assists you with arranging your promotional exercises, guaranteeing that nothing becomes lost despite any effort to the contrary.

2. Coordination: A promotional schedule guarantees that different showcasing channels and strategies are composed to create a durable brand message.

3. Planning: It permits you to design showcasing efforts around key occasions, seasons, or item dispatches.

4. Visibility: Colleagues can undoubtedly see forthcoming errands and cutoff times, encouraging straightforwardness and responsibility.

5. Efficiency: A very organized schedule smoothes out showcasing endeavors and decreases last-minute surges.

Building Your marketing schedule

Making a powerful advertising schedule includes a few stages:

1. Characterize Your Time Frame: Settle the period your showcasing schedule will cover. Most organizations anticipate a yearly or quarterly premise.

2. Distinguish Key Dates and Events: Recognize significant dates, occasions, and seasons that apply to your business. These will act as anchors for promoting efforts.

3. Set Objectives: Characterize the showcasing targets you intend to accomplish during the schedule; these targets will direct your preparation.

4. Select Showcasing Channels and Tactics: Figure out which promoting channels and strategies you'll use to accomplish your targets. Normal channels incorporate online entertainment, and email showcases show content.

5. Make a Substance Plan: Foster a substance plan that frames the subjects, topics, and sorts of content you'll make and distribute through the scheduled period.

6. Dole out Rscheduledilities: Appoint responsibilities regarding each promoting movement to explicit colleagues, guaranteeing responsibility.

7. Set Deadlines: Lay out cutoff times for each advertising assignment or mission, guaranteeing that they line up with your goals and key dates.

8. Screen and Adjust: Routinely audit and change your promotional schedule depending on the situation.

Be ready to adjust to changing conditions or arising concerns with consistency and Adaptability.

An effective showcasing schedule finds some kind of harmony between adaptability and adaptability. While it's vital to plan and execute advertising exercises reliably, you ought to likewise stay sufficiently adaptable to adjust to unforeseen occasions or new open doors.

Consistency: Consistency in promoting memorability and trust Guarantee that your image-informing and planning components stay predictable across all showcasing channels.

Flexibility: Be prepared to change your showcasing schedule to immediately jump all over surprising chances or address unexpected difficulties. Having alternate courses of action set up can assist you with adjusting successfully.

Instruments and Programming

Different instruments and programming are accessible to help you make and deal with your showcasing schedule. Well-known choices include:

1. Schedule Apps: Utilize advanced schedule applications like Google Schedule or Microsoft Viewpoint to make and impart showcasing schedules to your group.

2. Marketing Schedule Software: Particular advertising schedule programming can give more elements and customization choices for your showcasing arranging needs.

3. Project The Executives: Venture the board with apparatuses like Trello, Asana, or Monday. com can help you sort out and follow advertising errands and tasks.

4. Content Administration Frameworks (CMS): Assuming substance promotion is a huge piece
of your procedure, consider utilizing a CMS that incorporates content booking and distributing highlights.

A very organized promotional device is a vital device for dominating showcasing. It guarantees that your promoting exercises are arranged, coordinated, and executed, assisting you with accomplishing your targets and making a firm brand presence.

By finding some kind of harmony between consistency and adaptability, you'll be ready to explore the unique scene of showcasing.

In the parts that follow, we'll investigate extra parts of dominating showcasing, including client commitment, criticism circles, and persistent improvement. How about we proceed with our excursion in Part 10, where we'll dig into the specialty of client commitment and building enduring associations with your crowd?

CONCLUSION

Dominating marketing for Success

In the excursion of dominating and promoting, we've investigated an extensive cluster of procedures, strategies, and rules that are fundamental for outcomes in the present unique business scene. From creating a convincing brand character to making powerful marketing plans, and from the specialty of narrating to proficient asset distribution, we've covered the pivotal components that make up the advertiser's tool compartment.

All through this book, we've underlined the significance of adjusting and advancing. Showcasing is certainly not a static undertaking but a dynamic and consistently evolving field

To remain on top of things, advertisers should constantly embrace advancement, adjust to moving shoppers' ways of behaving, and influencing rising innovations and patterns.

Here are a few critically important points from our investigation:

1. Know Your Audience: Understanding your interest group profoundly is the groundwork for viable promotion. Purchaser personas and crowd research are significant instruments for interfacing with your clients on a significant level.

2. Craft Your Image Identity: Your image personality is something beyond a logo; it's the quintessence of your business. A solid brand personality ought to be steady across all touchpoints and mirror your guiding principle.

3. Tell Convincing Stories: Narrating is an integral asset for building profound associations

with your audience. Use stories to pass on your image's message and values.

4. Innovate or Stagnate: Development is a critical driver of progress in showcasing. Embrace groundbreaking thoughts, advances, and methodologies to remain cutthroat.

5. Plan Effectively: A very organized showcasing plan is fundamental for directing your endeavors and guaranteeing arrangements with business targets. Use advertising schedules to keep up with association and consistency.

6. Budget Wisely: carefully plan and allot your advertising spending plan to enhance your profit from the venture. Be ready to change your spending plan depending on the situation given execution and open doors.

7. Engage Your Audience: It is indispensable to Assemble and keep up with client connections. Draw in with your crowd through different channels, pay attention to their criticism, and offer some benefit reliably.

8. Measure, Investigate, and improve: Constantly screen and examine the exhibition of promotional endeavors. Use information-driven experiences to pursue informed choices and refine your methodologies.

9. Stay Adaptable: The promotion scene is continuously advancing.
Be prepared to adjust to changes in buyer conduct, economic situations, and innovation.

10. Never Stop Learning: Promoting is a unique field, and there's something else to learn. Remain inquisitive, search out new information, and put resources into your proficient turn of events.

Dominating showcasing is a continuous excursion, and achievement requires devotion, imagination, and a readiness to learn and develop. By applying the standards and methodologies examined in this book, you'll be better prepared to explore the steadily changing showcasing scene, associate with your crowd, and accomplish your business objectives.

Keep in mind that promoting isn't just about selling items or administrations; it's tied in with making encounters, taking care of issues, and having a constructive outcome on the existence of your clients.
As you proceed with your promotional venture, keep your crowd at the focal point of your endeavors, and let your enthusiasm for development and imagination drive you toward progress.

Much obliged to you for setting out on this excursion of dominating and promoting with us.

We wish you to proceed with the outcome in the entirety of your showcasing attempts, and may your image flourish in the always-advancing universe of advertising